D0578643

The Northwoods
TABLE

NATURAL CUISINE FEATURING NATIVE FOODS

The Northwoods TABLE

NATURAL CUISINE FEATURING NATIVE FOODS

By Henry Sinkus

Photography by Ron Modra

WILLOW CREEK PRESS

Minocqua, Wisconsin

Published by Willow Creek Press
P.O. Box 147
Minocqua, Wisconsin 54548

For information on other Willow Creek titles, call 1-800-850-9453

Library of Congress Cataloging-in-Publication Data

Sinkus, Henry.
   The Northwoods table : natural cuisine featuring native foods
/ by Henry Sinkus ; photography by Ron C. Modra.
      p. cm.
   ISBN 1-57223-291-9
   1. Cookery, American. I. Title.
TX715.S623 2000
641.5973--dc21   00-026387

Printed in Canada

Table of Contents

Introduction

My mother taught me to cook and instilled in me a passion for excellence. My work for major corporations over thirty years exposed me to cultures throughout the world, allowing me to study various cuisines and culinary techniques. I continue my studies every day, experimenting in my own kitchen and carefully watching the work of "The Great Chefs." What a perfect recipe for a second-career gourmet chef and caterer.

In 1993, my wife, Mary, and I purchased a small restaurant in Manitowish Waters, Wisconsin, a small resort community in the far northern part of the state. Armed with our dream, a willingness to work very hard and an incredible amount of determination, we established the Pine Baron's, a center-of-the-plate, white tablecloth dining establishment.

Our menu consists of many products found in the northern tier of the U.S., some wild, some cultivated. Our approach to food presentation combines these products with classic techniques, giving birth to what we call Northwoods Cuisine.

I encourage you to be creative in your culinary endeavors and to add a large amount of love to each of your creations. Food is an art form. The plate is your canvas; your paint, the products of the earth. Achieving success is akin to experiencing a spectacular Northwoods sunset or Mother Nature's display of the northern lights. Each time will be different and more beautiful than the last.

—Henry Sinkus
Manitowish Waters, WI

Northwoods Cuisine

Try to pin-point "Up North" on a United States map. A difficult task, even when equipped with a full box of push pins. Better, choose a forest-green colored marker and shade in the places we think of as "Up North" or the Northwoods.

Begin by cross-hatching parts of California's Redwood Forest and extend with bold strokes through the Columbia River Gorge in Oregon up to the snow-capped peaks of Washington State's North Cascades. Color-in around Cour d'Alene, Idaho, then skip over to Northern Minnesota, Northern Wisconsin, and Michigan's Upper Peninsula. Fill them all in. Reach out to the tip of New England and make sweeping swirls through most of Maine, with special attention to the jagged Northern Coast. Scribble through New Hampshire's Franconia Notch and Vermont's Lake Champlain, and color upstate New York's Adirondacks until the ink runs dry.

That's The Northwoods. On the map, anyway.

The different regions, all answering to the name, "Northwoods," are grouped together due to their similarities. All are distinguished by thickly-forested terrain and abundant wildlife. All are held in awe, even feared for their frequently harsh weather, especially during the long winters. People who choose to live here lead a robust life in a rugged land.

Ironically, the Northwoods is also a place of great peace, serenity and comfort. This claim can be made partly because in the Northwoods, one can disappear, wrapped into a blanket of trees and lakes. It's the beauty of a soothing sunset or the quiet of a fresh snowfall. It's the warmth of getting dry after a storm and coming inside to the most satisfying source of comfort "Up North" has to offer: its food.

By definition, Northwoods meals are comfort food: hot, hearty and filling. The climate demands it. Would a burly logger who worked all day in a driving Pacific Northwest rain choose fruit cup for his dinner? Would canoeists who paddled 21 miles through Minnesota's Boundary Waters slice celery sticks for their evening meal? Not likely. "Up North" they want it warm. They want it satisfying. And sometimes, as with the canoeists, logistics are a consideration. There may be no fresh celery to be had.

Early settlers dealt with such limitations, both of the region (what was grown or available there) and their era (no refrigeration, microwaves, or supermarkets). Certain Northwoods' specialties, which remain popular today, were created because they were practical.

One such specialty is the pasty, (pronounced with a soft "a"), a meat, potato and vegetable-filled portable pie which Cornish miners brought to Michigan's upper peninsula in the mid-1800s. Pasties were hearty and held up in the mines much better than your average sandwich.

Another lasting Northwoods' tradition is the Friday Fish Fry, which originated in heavily Catholic areas. Many Catholics didn't eat meat on Fridays (some still don't), especially during Lent. Today, families form lines out the door at restaurants in Bemidji, Minnesota, or Grand Marais, Michigan. It's less about religion and more about the heaping, all-you-can-eat platters of fried fish, accompanied by french fries, hush puppies and cole slaw.

A close cousin of the fish fry is the fish boil, a still wildly popular event in places such as Door County, Wisconsin (the peninsula along Lake Michigan). Fish Boils are a Scandinavian tradition dating back to 19th century lumberjacks. Huge kettles are filled with walleye, cod, or northern pike and placed over wood fires. After onions and potatoes are added, the "boilmaster" throws kerosene over the fire, the pot boils over and it's chow time. (Save room for cherry pie.)

Another fish fry offshoot is the shore lunch. What began as fishermen merely pulling their boats to shore to cook their catch has become a quaint and popular tradition. A shore lunch is actually a picnic where fish is either fried, barbecued or baked, usually alongside the lake or river where a group has been fishing. There's nothing more mouth-watering and satisfying than cooking and eating just-caught salmon, lake trout, walleye or clams.

Another distinctive characteristic of Northwoods cooking is the "fish or game" component. Fishing and hunting is part of life "Up North." Years ago, for Native Americans and early white settlers, fishing and hunting meant survival. Today, fishing and hunting are enjoyable outdoor pastimes with a bonus of great tasting fresh food. Open any Northwoods freezer — there will be venison or some kind of fish which a neighbor brought or the homeowner caught.

The Northwoods provides other local specialties which are part of its hardy heritage. Wild rice, a staple of the early and current Native American diet, is now a common sight in Minnesota gift stores and in gourmet gift baskets. And cranberries. They're not just for Thanksgiving anymore.

Things are different today. There is overnight shipping for fresh produce or non-local fish. Storage and freezing capabilities are top-notch. Today, Northwoods' cooks have the opportunity to blend the best of the traditional and local with advanced techniques and new, exotic, imported ingredients.

We call it Northwoods Cuisine.

In 1993, Mary and Henry Sinkus established The Pine Baron's Restaurant in Manitowish Waters, Wisconsin, a tiny lakeside wedge of paradise way Up North. The Sinkuses are both retired communications executives who traded their cell phones, beepers, and always-packed suitcases for the more gratifying, if not exactly relaxing, business of running a dining establishment. They wanted to create a casual but elegant place serving the most delicious food they could imagine. Henry, the Pine Baron's chef and author of these recipes, wanted to feature Northwoods Cuisine.

"To me, Northwoods Cuisine means using native, historically-used products and taking them to a new dimension," Henry says. "Essentially, reinventing them for the demands of today's more sophisticated diner."

Henry's idea is to take classical techniques and build on them, trying new twists. Always with an eye for presentation. Try blackberries with port wine when grilling a rack of venison or beef. Stuff a pasty with chopped rather than ground ingredients and finish the crust with an elegant seal (since this pasty is unlikely to go home in a miner's pocket).

Before settling Up North, the Sinkuses traveled extensively and lived in many places including Detroit, San Francisco, Chicago, Honolulu, Philadelphia, Germany, France and Spain. They discovered many ingredients during their travels which appear in Henry's recipes. For example, the Venison Spring Roll recipe combines a Northwoods' staple, cranberry syrup, with a Thai-style garlic chili pepper sauce. It's all about the flavor.

Henry's upbringing was another source of inspiration for these recipes. His mother taught him to cook classic Lithuanian dishes such as Kastinas, or Sour Cream Butter, which is spread over potatoes or bread. The Lithuanian influence is evident in original creations such as the delicious Wild Mushroom Crisps, which look like a pizza with a potato crust.

Henry, who never took a cooking class, attributes his skills (after proper credit for mom), to 20 years of experimentation and watching chefs such as Julia Child on PBS and the Discovery Channel. Henry, who uses a ruler to keep his place when following a recipe, approaches cooking with the discipline and clarity of his former vocation: engineering.

"Cooking is an art form, absolutely," he says. "But it's also like an engineering plan. Start with an objective. Then develop a plan to get there. A recipe is like a road map to get to your main objective."

The objective of this book is to guide and inspire you to set a Northwoods table. The ingredients and combinations should enable any cook to create the ambiance of a log cabin with a fire crackling in a pot-bellied stove. The aromas, the succulent tastes will all be there. You provide the birch trees just outside the window, with their green leaves shimmering in the sun. Or a fresh, crunchy snowfall. Or the bleeding reds and burning yellows of Fall maple trees. Season is optional.

Pull out the white tablecloth, or the tin campfire plates. It will be Northwoods Cuisine just the same.

Soups

Cold Beet Soup

In this refreshing chilled soup, the oft-neglected beet is finally given its due. Instead of being sliced and served as a lonely side dish, the beets in this recipe provide the rosy pink color and tangy flavor of the perfect first course for any summer menu.

In a large stainless steel bowl or 4-quart stockpot, blend together the sour cream and beet juice. Slowly incorporate the beef or vegetable stock, then blend in the heavy cream and vinegar. Add beets, cucumber, chives and dill, and mix gently. Refrigerate at least two hours before serving.

This soup should be piquant and slightly sweet in taste. Adjust seasoning with salt and additional vinegar if required.

Serves six to eight.

2 15-ounce cans diced beets, drained,
   juice reserved
8 ounces sour cream
1 quart beef or vegetable stock
8 ounces heavy cream
⅓ cup white vinegar
3 Tablespoons minced chives
1 medium cucumber, peeled, seeded
   and julienne sliced
2 to 3 Tablespoons minced fresh dill

Cabbage Bisque

The underrated cabbage is transformed into a fresh, nutty and creamy bisque. Serve with a salad of field greens with cranberry mustard vinaigrette and crusty fresh bread.

In a 4-quart stockpot, melt the butter and sauté the onion and carrot for 3 to 5 minutes (do not allow to brown). Add the cabbage and mix thoroughly. Sauté over low heat for 5 minutes.

In a 1-quart saucepan, melt 3 Tablespoons sweet butter. Add ¼cup flour and whisk constantly to achieve a light brown roux. Slowly add 2 cups vegetable stock. Stir constantly until thickened.

Add remaining 4 cups vegetable stock to the sautéed cabbage mixture. Add the roux mixture, cream and nutmeg and simmer until heated through. Adjust seasoning to taste with salt and freshly ground pepper.

Serves six to eight.

1 pound sweet butter
½ cup minced onion
½ cup finely shredded carrot
1 pound finely shredded cabbage (commercially prepared cabbage cole slaw mix works very well)
3 Tablespoons sweet butter
¼ cup flour
2-quarts vegetable stock
2 cups heavy cream
1 teaspoon nutmeg

Cream of Wild Mushroom Soup

Imagine the flavor and earthy aroma of mushrooms fresh from the forest floor and the sweetness of onion blended with sherry, cream and a hint of nutmeg — a soup for the soul.

In a 4-quart stockpot, melt the butter and sauté the onion until translucent. Add the mushrooms and sauté for 10 to 15 minutes, stirring occasionally.

In a 1-quart saucepan, melt 3 Tablespoons sweet butter. Add ¼ cup flour and whisk constantly to achieve a light brown roux. Slowly add 2 cups chicken stock. Stir constantly until thickened.

Add remaining 4 cups chicken stock to the sautéed mushrooms and onions. Add the roux mixture and cream and simmer until heated through. Add sherry and nutmeg. Adjust seasoning to taste with salt and freshly ground pepper.

Serves six to eight.

½ pound sweet butter
1 small onion, diced
2 cups domestic mushrooms, thickly sliced (about ⅛")
2 cups wild mushrooms (shiitaki, portobello, seps, etc. Domestic mushrooms may be substituted), thickly sliced (about ⅛")
3 Tablespoons sweet butter
¼ cup flour
6 cups chicken stock
2 cups heavy cream
2 Tablespoons sherry
¼ teaspoon nutmeg

Cream of Asparagus Soup

Soups and stews have long been Northwoods' staples. They are as soothing to prepare as they are to eat. This creamy soup is soon to be found simmering in Dutch ovens from the Adirondacks all the way to Mount Hood.

In a 4-quart stockpot, cook asparagus stems in 4 cups stock over medium heat. Cook until tender. Purée the cooked asparagus stems and stock with a hand blender or in a food processor.

In another stockpot, melt the butter. Blend in the flour and stir in the asparagus purée. Simmer over low heat 3-4 minutes, stirring constantly. Add the cream.

In a saucepan, bring the remaining 2 cups stock to a boil. Blanch the asparagus tips and add, with liquid, to the stockpot mixture. Season with nutmeg, salt and pepper. Serve hot or cold.

Serves eight.

4 cups asparagus tips
4 cups asparagus stems cut in ½" pieces
6 cups chicken or vegetable stock
6 Tablespoons butter
4 Tablespoons flour
3 cups heavy cream
⅛ teaspoon nutmeg
salt and pepper to taste

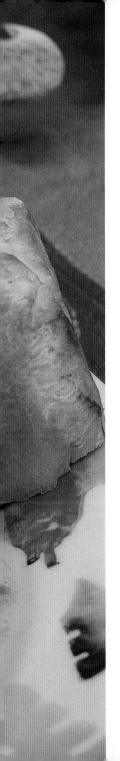

Cream of Wild Rice Soup

Wild rice, still considered somewhat exotic in many parts of the country, is a Northwoods' staple. Indians depended on it for centuries. Today, wild rice is better known but still a bit misunderstood. This "rice" is actually a grain, very similar to barley. The cooked product produces a rich, nutty and earthy taste. The perfect base for this satisfying soup.

In a 4-quart stockpot, melt the butter and sauté the onion until translucent. Add the flour to make a light brown roux. Slowly add the chicken stock and blend thoroughly. Add the cooked wild rice, sherry and heavy cream. Simmer 15 minutes or until heated through. Season to taste with salt and freshly ground pepper.

Serves six to eight.

For added interest, add any of the following:
 ½ cup chopped ham
 1 cup sliced wild mushrooms
 ½ cup grated carrots

¼ **pound sweet butter**
1 small onion, diced
¼ **cup flour**
4 cups chicken stock
2 cups cooked wild rice★
2 Tablespoons dry sherry
2 cups heavy cream

★ Wild Rice:
One cup uncooked wild rice yields four cups cooked.
In a fine strainer, rinse rice under cold water. Place the rice in a heavy saucepan and add 4 cups of water for each cup of rice. Heat to boiling, cover and simmer over low heat for 40 to 50 minutes, until grains begin to split or rice is tender.

Potato Soup

The sturdy spud is another of the Northwoods' staples. Historically, potatoes were stored in cellars in heaping quantities and eaten throughout the long winters and into the summer months. This soup pulls the potato from the chorus line and makes it the simmering star of the show.

In a deep soup kettle, melt the butter and sauté bacon until translucent. Add the onion and cook until soft. Blend in the flour and slowly add stock, stirring constantly. Add the potatoes and simmer for one hour.

In a stainless steel bowl, whisk the egg yolks and blend in the sour cream. Temper the mixture by slowly mixing in 2 cups hot broth. Add this mixture to the soup and simmer 10 to 15 minutes. Do not boil. Purée approximately one third of the soup with a hand blender or in a food processor and return to the pot. Serve immediately, garnished with fresh minced parsley or chives.

Serves eight.

¼ **pound butter**
12 slices bacon, cut into ¼" strips
3 large onions, finely chopped
5 Tablespoons flour
10 cups chicken stock or bouillon
8 medium to large red potatoes, scrubbed and diced
4 egg yolks
2 cups sour cream

Venison Chili

Across the north, heart-warming, belly-filling chili is appreciated by lumberjacks, cross-country skiers, and small town mayors alike. This chili starts with lean venison to provide a woodsy taste. If you've got the time, simmer this chili for several hours to develop the subtle flavors.

In a heavy 4-quart stockpot, heat olive oil. Dust venison with flour and brown quickly in hot oil. Remove venison. Melt butter in stockpot and sauté onion, garlic and green pepper for 6 to 8 minutes, stirring occasionally. Add orange juice and deglaze the pan. Add chili powder, cumin and tomatoes and simmer for 10 minutes. Add venison and beans. Mix thoroughly, reduce heat and simmer 1 hour, stirring occasionally. If chili gets too thick, add additional orange juice. Stir in ½ cup Thai chili pepper sauce. Adjust seasoning with salt and additional Thai chili pepper sauce. Serve with steamed rice and crusty French bread.

Serves six to eight generously.

2 pounds venison, cut in 1" cubes (beef may be substituted)
2 Tablespoons flour
⅓ cup olive oil
¼ pound sweet butter
2 cups chopped onion
2 cups chopped green pepper
1 Tablespoon minced garlic
1 cup orange juice
2½ Tablespoons chili powder
½ Tablespoon ground cumin
3 16-ounce cans stewed tomatoes, puréed in food processor
3 cups cooked 7-bean mix
½ to 1 cup Thai chili pepper sauce

Appetizers and Side Dishes

Wild Mushroom Crisps

These hors d'oeuvres are Lithuanian-inspired potato pancakes taken to a new dimension. The crisps eat like pieces of pizza topped with flavorful wild mushrooms, one of the earthiest ingredients found "Up North."

Reconstitute mushrooms in sherry wine. Drain well.

Season potatoes with salt and pepper. Melt 2 ounces sweet butter in a 7-inch skillet over medium-high heat. Add potatoes, forming a level round disc. Fry 3 to 4 minutes per side or until crispy and brown. Remove from pan and drain on paper towel.

To assemble, spread cream cheese on potato crisp. Arrange mushrooms, and top with fresh tomato. Sprinkle minced herbs and cheese on top.

Place the crisp on a baking sheet and cook in a 350° oven for 3 to 5 minutes or until cheese melts.

Serves two as an appetizer.

1½ cup fresh shredded potato (1 large potato)

2 ounces butter

1 ounce cream cheese, softened

6 to 8 dried wild mushrooms (domestic mushrooms may be substituted)

fresh tomato slices

shredded asiago or mozzarella cheese

minced fresh herbs – basil, dill, cilantro

Walleye and Crayfish Mousseline

Fishermen from Michigan to the many lakes of Wisconsin and Minnesota name the tender and flaky walleye as the best eating fish. This recipe is somewhat involved, but well worth the time and effort.

Preheat oven to 400°. Lightly butter an 11" x 4" paté terrine and the cover, or use a loaf pan. Cut a piece of parchment or waxed paper to line the inside of the cover and butter the paper.

Place walleye filet in food processor bowl fitted with knife blade. Process until coarsely chopped, about 20 seconds. Add crayfish and process for an additional 20 seconds. Add pistachios and process for approximately 10 seconds more until well blended. Add celery salt, white pepper, paprika, onion powder, garlic powder, oregano, black pepper and sherry. Process for approximately 10 seconds until well blended. With food processor on, slowly add cream and process until the mixture is amalgamated into a smooth paste, approximately 30 seconds.

Spoon mixture into the buttered paté terrine, packing well and smoothing the top with a spoon or spatula. Cover the top with the parchment paper and place the lid on the terrine. Place terrine in a deep baking pan. Fill pan with water to ⅔ the height of the terrine. Bake for 40 minutes or until internal temperature of the mousseline is 180°. Remove terrine from water bath to cooling rack – carefully remove lid and parchment paper. When cool, unmold mousse, wrap in plastic wrap and refrigerate for at least 1 hour, preferably overnight.

For service, slice ¼" thick with an electric knife. Present 2 to 3 slices per serving on a bed of salad greens with mayonnaise seasoned with cayenne pepper to taste.

Serves six to eight as an hor d'ouvre.

28 ounces skinned walleye filet (ocean perch, cod flounder or sole may be substituted)
11 ounces cooked or raw crayfish meat
¼ cup shelled, roasted pistachios
1½ teaspoons celery salt
1 teaspoon white pepper
½ teaspoon sweet paprika
½ teaspoon onion powder
½ teaspoon garlic powder
½ teaspoon ground oregano
½ teaspoon black pepper
3 Tablespoons sherry
1 cup heavy cream

Mousseline of Morels, Yellow Squash, Fiddlehead Fern and Roasted Red Pepper

This dish is proof-positive that food is an art form. Among the artist's media here: the exotic, coiled fiddlehead fern found in the woods in springtime (or in a gourmet grocery or from a mail-order supply house).

Aspic mixture:

In a 1-quart stainless steel bowl, dissolve 1 Tablespoon unflavored gelatin in ¼ cup cold water. Add ½ cup boiling chicken or vegetable stock and stir until dissolved. Add ¼ cup tomato juice, 1 cup additional stock, 1 Tablespoon lemon juice and 1 teaspoon lemon zest.

Assembly:

Lightly oil a 9" x 5" loaf pan. Line with plastic wrap extending 6" on all sides.

Select best appearing cabbage leaves. Line the loaf pan with the cabbage leaves. Layer vegetables as follows:

Layer 1: morel mushrooms	*Layer 5: morel mushrooms*
Layer 2: roasted red pepper	*Layer 6: roasted red pepper*
Layer 3: fiddlehead fern	*Layer 7: fiddlehead fern*
Layer 4: roasted yellow squash	*Layer 8: roasted yellow squash*

Ladle aspic mixture over vegetables to fill the pan. Fold cabbage leaves over top of the vegetables. Fold plastic wrap over the top to cover. Weight down with heavy plate or plastic bottle filled with water. Refrigerate overnight.

Remove from pan and carefully remove plastic wrap. Slice with electric knife into 1" slices and serve with Curried Mayonnaise.

Serves eight.

Curried Mayonnaise:

Dissolve 1 teaspoon madras curry powder or Thai red curry paste in 1 Tablespoon hot water. Blend into 1 cup mayonnaise. Chill at least one hour before serving.

Aspic:

1 Tablespoon unflavored gelatin

1½ cups chicken or vegetable stock

¼ cup tomato juice

1 Tablespoon lemon juice

1 teaspoon lemon zest

1 large head cabbage leaves, blanched, stems removed

6 red peppers, roasted, peeled and seeded

½ pound fiddlehead fern, blanched (or asparagus tips)

3 yellow squash, cut lengthwise in ¼" strips and roasted in a buttered pan for 10 minutes at 300°

½ pound morel mushrooms, blanched and cut in half

Venison Spring Roll

A labor of love, this appetizer presentation will dazzle your guests. It will also introduce them to the wonderful flavors and textures of venison, a cholesterol-free red meat familiar to and beloved by Northwoods' natives.

Heat 2 ounces clarified butter in a heavy skillet. Add venison and quickly sear to rare. Drain well and place in mixing bowl. Add teriyaki sauce, Madeira wine, celery salt and white pepper. Mix well and marinate at least 30 minutes.

Place sun-dried tomatoes in a small bowl. Cover with ¼ cup warm demi-glace and let stand for 30 minutes to reconstitute. Drain well.

Blanch carrots in boiling water for 1 minute. Plunge into ice water, drain and pat dry with towel. Sauté onion, celery and garlic in 1 ounce clarified butter until caramelized. Drain well. Sauté shiitake mushrooms in 1 ounce clarified butter until slightly limp.

Combine the marinated venison, pine nuts, reconstituted sun-dried tomatoes, carrot, onion mixture and shiitake mushrooms. Mix well.

Place egg roll wrappers on work surface. Place an equal amount of the venison mixture in the center if each wrapper. Fold one corner of the wrapper over the filling. Fold in the two sides and wrap the filling. Moisten the top edge of the wrapper with egg wash to seal. Rolls should be about 4" long.

For cranberry dipping sauce, heat 2 cups demi-glace with the Madeira wine, cranberry syrup and chili pepper sauce. Simmer 2 to 3 minutes, stirring occasionally. Keep warm.

Preheat vegetable oil in deep skillet to 340°. Fry spring rolls for 3 to 4 minutes or until golden brown and heated through. Drain well and serve immediately.

Presentation:

Nap plate with cranberry dipping sauce. Slice spring rolls in half diagonally. Arrange four pieces on plate. Garnish with whole cranberry sauce.

½ **pound venison or beef tenderloin (sliced ⅜" thick; cut in ⅜" wide strips)**
2 **teaspoons teriyaki sauce**
1 **teaspoon Madeira wine**
¼ **teaspoon celery salt**
⅛ **teaspoon white pepper**
3 **Tablespoons sun-dried tomato (cut in ⅛" strips)**
¼ **cup demi-glaze**
¼ **cup carrot (sliced in ⅛" strips, 2" long)**
¼ **cup sweet onion (thinly sliced)**
¼ **cup celery (sliced in ⅛" strips, 2" long)**
2 **cloves garlic (finely chopped)**
4 **ounces clarified sweet butter**
½ **cup shiitake mushroom (sliced in ⅛" strips)**
¼ **cup toasted pine nuts**
8 **large egg roll wrappers (6½" x 6½")**
4 **cups vegetable oil**

Cranberry Dipping Sauce:
2 **cups demi-glace**
1 **ounce Madeira wine**
2 **Tablespoons cranberry syrup**
2 **teaspoons Thai-style garlic chili pepper sauce**
whole cranberry sauce for garnish

Marinated Mussel Salad

There are two secrets to this salad: finding the freshest Maine mussels from under the rough and tumble Atlantic, and steaming them until they open and pull away from the shell (about 4 minutes). Do Not Overcook!

In a 2-quart saucepan, heat the butter and olive oil. Add onion, garlic and green pepper and sauté 5 minutes or until onions are opaque. Add tomato and spices. Simmer for 10 minutes. Adjust seasoning with salt and pepper. Transfer to a stainless steel or ceramic bowl. Stir in black olives and capers.

Remove mussel meat from shells. Add mussels to tomato mixture and stir well. Refrigerate overnight. Serve over fresh field greens.

Serves six to eight.

For Marinated Mussels on the half shell:
Reserve the bottom half of each mussel shell and serve mussels on the shell as an appetizer.

4 pounds fresh black mussels, steamed with 1 Tablespoon garlic, 1 Tablespoon seafood seasoning and white wine
2 Tablespoons sweet butter
1 Tablespoon olive oil
2 Tablespoons chopped garlic
1 cup finely chopped onion
1 cup finely chopped green pepper
2 16-ounce cans stewed tomatoes, finely chopped
1 teaspoon chopped fresh basil
1 teaspoon chopped fresh oregano
2 Tablespoons Thai chili pepper sauce or ½ teaspoon cayenne pepper mixed with 1 Tablespoon ketchup and 1 Tablespoon molasses
3½ cups sliced black olives
1 Tablespoon capers

Potatoes Stuffed with Wild Mushrooms

Something special to accompany chops or steaks, or perhaps a late snack or vegetarian meal. Either way, wild mushrooms bump up the flavor in this exceptional side dish.

Bake potatoes until skins are crisp. With a serrated knife, cut the top third from each potato. Scoop out the centers, reserving the shells, and mash. Combine the mashed potato with the chopped mushroom, chives, dill, egg, heavy cream and nutmeg. (To cook dried wild mushrooms, saute in butter until softened.) Refill the shells with this mixture.

Arrange the potatoes in a lightly-buttered baking dish. Top with sour cream. Sprinkle liberally with cheese and bread crumbs. Garnish with a whole mushroom. Bake in a preheated 300° oven for 10 – 15 minutes or until heated through.

Serves four.

4 baking potatoes
½ cup cooked, dried wild mushrooms, finely chopped (domestic mushrooms may be substituted)
1 Tablespoon finely minced fresh chives
1 beaten egg
2–3 Tablespoons heavy cream
pinch of nutmeg
1 cup sour cream
1 teaspoon dill weed, shredded
bread crumbs, asiago or white cheddar cheese and melted butter for topping
4 whole cooked, dried wild mushrooms for garnish

Stewed Pumpkin and Apples

A delicious accompaniment to fall and winter menus, this side dish is a cornucopia of the reds and oranges of autumn leaves in full burst. The craisins — dried cranberries which are intensely sweet and chewy enough to eat as a snack — provide the zip of this dish.

Bring water to boil in a 2-quart saucepan. Add pumpkin and cook until a fork or skewer can be inserted without resistance. Drain pumpkin, toss together with apples and craisins and transfer to an oven-proof casserole.

In a 1-quart saucepan, melt the butter. Add ginger, brown sugar and Cointreau and heat until the sugar is dissolved. Season with salt and pepper and pour over pumpkin apple mixture. Bake, uncovered, in a preheated 300° oven for 30 to 40 minutes or until apples are semi-soft. Dot each serving with a pat of butter.

Serves four to six.

*To create Pumpkin Apple Bisque, process the mixture with 1 quart heavy cream and 2 cups chicken or vegetable stock in a food processor or blender. Salt and pepper to taste.

4 cups fresh pumpkin or squash, peeled and cut into 1" cubes
1 quart water
4 cups Granny Smith apples, cored and cut into 1" cubes
2 Tablespoons craisins (dried cranberries) or raisins
⅓ cup sweet butter
2 ounces Cointreau
½ cup dark brown sugar
salt and pepper to taste
pinch of ground or fresh ginger

Fiddlehead Fern and Wild Mushroom Timbales

Another gourmet delight with ingredients fresh from the nearest Northwoods forest floor. Traditional custard encases crisp fiddleheads and morels forming an appealing timbale, or 3-inch tall mold. There is a magician in the kitchen.

In a stainless steel bowl, beat the eggs and slowly add the cream. Add salt, paprika and nutmeg.

Lightly butter eight 6-ounce ramekins. Place 3 fiddlehead ferns in the bottom of each, then a morel mushroom (cut in half), then 3 more fiddlehead ferns. Fill the ramekins ⅔ full with the egg and cream mixture.

Place the ramekins on a rack in a deep baking pan. Fill the pan with hot water to ⅔ the height of the ramekins.

Bake in a preheated 325° oven for 20-30 minutes until a knife inserted in the center comes out clean. Cool the timbales and chill for several hours.

To serve, unmold on a bed of greens.

Serves eight.

1½ cups heavy cream or 1 cup heavy cream and ½ cup chicken stock
4 eggs (room temperature)
¾ teaspoon salt
½ teaspoon paprika
pinch nutmeg
8 morel mushrooms
48 fiddlehead ferns (or asparagus tips)

Malfade (Spinach Rolls)

For early Northwoods settlers, vegetables were a rarity, grown, cooked and eaten during the brief summers. Today, from Presque Isle, Maine, to Presque Isle, Wisconsin, there is no excuse for skipping your greens, especially when they're folded into this elegant, versatile dish — a spinach roll with marinara sauce, cheese and mushrooms. Serve as a first course, an entrée, or on the side.

To prepare white sauce, melt butter over low heat in a 1-quart saucepan. Slowly whisk in the flour, stirring constantly for 2 to 3 minutes. Slowly whisk in the cream. Season to taste. Continue stirring until sauce is silky and thick. Remove from heat and cool slightly.

To prepare the spinach roll, mix together spinach, bread crumbs, eggs, salt and pepper in a stainless steel bowl. Form into four ½ cup egg shapes. If mixture is too wet, add bread crumbs. If too dry, add beaten egg.

Butter four 6-inch oven-proof dishes that are at least 1½" deep, or one dish that will accomodate four spinach rolls. Ladle 4 ounces (½ cup) of marinara sauce in each dish. Place a spinach roll on the sauce and cover with white sauce. Arrange ¼ cup mushrooms in each dish and top with ¼ cup shredded cheese.

Bake in a preheated 300° oven for 15 to 20 minutes or until cheese is bubbly and browned.

Serves four.

Spinach roll:

2 cups blanched spinach, coarsely chopped
¼ cup seasoned bread crumbs
2 eggs, beaten
½ teaspoon salt
¼ teaspoon white pepper
1 cup domestic mushrooms, thickly sliced
1 - 1½ cups shredded asiago or mozzarella cheese
2 cups of your favorite marinara sauce (add meat if you're serving this as an entrée)

White sauce:

6 Tablespoons butter
6 Tablespoons flour
2 cups heavy cream
salt, pepper and nutmeg to taste

Marinated Fresh Vegetable Salad

Pluck the freshest vegetables from a lakeside farmer's market to make this crisp, refreshing salad. Definitely a departure from the ordinary.

In a stainless steel bowl, whisk together vinegar, olive oil and lemon juice. Add basil, salt and pepper. Let stand at least 20 minutes.

Arrange vegetables in a stainless steel or glass bowl. Add marinade and cover with plastic wrap. Refrigerate for 24 hours. Serve on a bed of fresh salad greens.

⅓ cup red wine vinegar
⅔ cup olive oil
1 Tablespoon lemon juice
¼ teaspoon basil
¼ teaspoon salt
⅛ teaspoon white pepper
2 cups asparagus tips
2 cups domestic mushrooms, thickly sliced
1½ cups plum tomatoes, seeded and ¾" diced
1½ cups zucchini squash, ¼" diced
2 cups artichoke hearts
2 to 3 Tablespoons capers (optional)
½ cup sliced black olives (optional)

Oven Roasted Rosemary Red Skin Potatoes

Simple techniques transform the lowly, sometimes boring, potato into a gourmet delight.

Place potatoes in single layer in a 1-quart oven-proof casserole. In a small saucepan, melt butter. Add rosemary and celery salt. Pour butter mixture over potatoes to coat well. Bake in 350° preheated oven for 15 minutes or until crisp and hot.

Serves six to eight.

4 cups "B" size red skin potatoes –
   quartered and blanched for 2
   minutes
1¼ pounds sweet butter
1 teaspoon ground rosemary
dash celery salt

Spicy Red Cabbage

In a 2-quart saucepan, mix together the vinegar, sugar and allspice. Bring to a boil and reduce heat to simmer. Add the onion, and simmer 5 minutes. Add the cabbage and apple and simmer until tender.

Serves six to eight.

1 small head red cabbage, cored and
   finely shredded
2 Granny Smith apples, cored, peeled
   and finely shredded
1 small onion, sliced very thin
¾ cup red wine vinegar
¾ cup sugar
pinch of allspice

Main Dishes

Spicy Roast Duckling with Raspberry Sauce

This succulent Northwoods duck is moist, juicy and virtually fat-free. The just-this-side-of-spicy seasonings are complemented and cooled by the tangy, more Northern than orange, raspberry sauce.

In a 3" deep roasting pan, build a nest of carrot and celery topped with sliced onion. Moisten the duck halves with a commercially-prepared, mild Louisiana-style hot sauce and place the halves atop the vegetables, skin side up. Dust the duck with 1 Tablespoon dry rub seasoning. Cover the pan with heavy duty aluminum foil and bake in a preheated 400° oven for 2 hours, 15 minutes.

Remove duck from oven and carefully remove foil, avoiding steam. Cool slightly and remove duck to platter. (Note: the fat in the pan can be saved and used for frying potatoes.) Discard the vegetables and any liquid remaining in pan. Cool the duck until it can be comfortably handled. Remove all bones from the body cavity. Wrap each half in plastic wrap and refrigerate overnight.

Prepare sauce by mixing the raspberry jam, sugar, water, Triple Sec and brandy in a 2-quart saucepan. Stirring constantly, bring the mixture to a boil. Reduce heat and simmer for 10 to 15 minutes, stirring occasionally. Strain the mixture into a clean 2-quart saucepan and return to low heat. Mix together cornstarch and teriyaki sauce. Add to raspberry jam mixture and heat until slightly thickened.

To serve, remove plastic wrap from duck. Place halves, skin side up, in a baking dish and heat in a 400° oven for 15 minutes. Baste with raspberry sauce and return to oven for 5 minutes.

Serves two.

1 duck, split and trimmed of all fat and excess skin
2 pieces carrot (5" long)
2 pieces celery (5" long)
1 cup thinly sliced onion

Dry Rub Seasoning
In a food processor, blend together the following:
2 Tablespoons salt
¼ cup dried onion
1 Tablespoon cayenne pepper
1 Tablespoon white pepper
2 Tablespoons paprika
2 Tablespoons dried basil
1 Tablespoon dry mustard
1 teaspoon ground cumin
1 Tablespoon granulated garlic

Raspberry Sauce
8-ounce jar raspberry jam
1 cup sugar
1 cup water
1 ounce Triple Sec
1 ounce raspberry brandy
½ cup teriyaki sauce
2 Tablespoons cornstarch

Semi-Boneless Grouse Stuffed with Morels and Wild Rice

The grouse is among the most sought-after of Northwoods game birds. The preparation of stuffed grouse is somewhat involved, but always worth the effort. If time is short on serving day, prepare the grouse ahead of time, wrap and freeze it. To cook from frozen, allow 15 to 20 minutes of additional cooking time.

In a saucepan, mix together glaze ingredients. Heat to simmer, stirring occasionally.

Remove the rib cage from the grouse with a very sharp boning knife by cutting along each side of the breast bone. Carefully cut the meat from both sides of the rib cage and pull the rib cage from the meat, being careful not to tear the skin. Remove the thigh bones. Season the boned cavity with salt and pepper and refrigerate for 20 minutes.

For stuffing, mix together wild rice, sautéed shallot, sun-dried tomato and butter. Add a few grains of nutmeg.

Lay a boned grouse, skin side down, on a cutting board. Arrange morels, cut side down, in the cavity, then cover with stuffing. Fold skin flaps around stuffing and shape into a round with legs pointing up. Wrap the round with bacon strip and secure with a toothpick. Bake in a preheated 350° oven for 20 to 30 minutes or until internal temperature is 160° to 180°. Ten minutes before serving, brush the glaze mixture onto the grouse and return to oven for 5 to 10 minutes.

1 8- to 14-ounce grouse per serving (may substitute Cornish game hen)
1 strip bacon per serving

Stuffing (per serving):
⅓ cup cooked wild rice*
1 teaspoon sautéed minced shallot
1 teaspoon softened sun-dried tomato, minced
1 Tablespoon sweet butter at room temperature
nutmeg
2 small morel mushrooms, cut in half (domestic mushrooms may be substituted)

Honey Teriyaki Glaze (per serving):
1 Tablespoon honey
1 Tablespoon white wine
1 teaspoon teriyaki sauce

* See page 21 for directions on cooking wild rice.

Cornish Pasties

Cornish miners who settled the Upper Peninsula of Michigan in the mid-1800s found this baked pocket easy to transport and perfect for "dining" in the cramped, hot iron mines. Originally, the pastry was made with lard, and meat was an insignificant ingredient in an economy where the average wage was less than $30 per month. This recipe is for a more formal party, complete with plenty of chopped meat, vegetables and a buttery short crust stamped with an elegant seal.

Pastry Dough:

In a food processor bowl fitted with a metal blade, cut the butter into the flour by pulsing the blade. Turn the machine on constant power and slowly add the ice water in a steady stream. In less than 30 seconds, a ball will form. Stop the machine. Divide the dough into 8 equal portions. Wrap each in plastic wrap and refrigerate for at least one hour.

Filling:

In a heavy skillet, heat the olive oil over medium heat. Dust the meat with flour, add to heated oil and brown on all sides. Remove to a stainless steel bowl. Deglaze the skillet with the wine and add the garlic, mustard and brown sugar. Pour this reduction over the meat and marinate at least one hour in the refrigerator.

Drain marinade from meat and reserve. Combine meat with vegetables.

Roll pastry dough into 7" rounds. Place one cup of the meat / vegetable mixture in the center. Spoon 2 Tablespoons marinade on top. Place second round on top, like a sandwich. Fold and crimp seal the pasty. Place pasties on baking sheet. Brush with cold water or egg wash. Cut a small vent in the top. Bake in a preheated 350° oven for 20 to 25 minutes or until golden brown.

Serves four.

Pastry Dough:
2⅔ cups flour
½ pound cold sweet butter, cut into small pieces
½ cup ice water

Filling:
1½ cups meat (venison, beef, pork etc.), cut in 1" cubes
2 Tablespoons flour
2 Tablespoons olive oil
½ cup white wine
¼ teaspoon minced garlic
1 Tablespoon Dijon mustard
1 teaspoon brown sugar
½ cup blanched diced turnip
½ cup blanched diced carrot
½ cup blanched diced rutabaga
½ cup par-boiled diced white potato
½ cup sautéed onion
1 cup sliced mushrooms

Hunters Wild Game Stew with Baked Pumpkin

"A bit of this and a bit of that" comes together in this earthy, "sit-around-the-fire-and-eat-every-bite" stew. Fruits of the year's harvest are combined with lean, flavorful venison to make a wonderful, hearty dish to prepare for family and friends on the chilly, snowy days of winter.

In a heavy 6- to 8-quart covered stockpot, melt the butter and quickly brown the venison, duck and pork separately. Drain meat on paper towel. Sauté onion, celery and garlic in butter for 5 minutes. Add wine and stock and deglaze the pan. Bring the liquid to a boil and add the meat and sausage. Reduce heat and simmer, covered, for 20 minutes. Add remaining ingredients and simmer, covered, for 1½ to 2 hours. (If you will be serving the stew in a pumpkin, reduce the simmer to ½ hour and proceed to the directions below.) Adjust seasoning with salt and pepper.

Serve the stew in bowls or over buttered noodles, garnishing with Baked Pumpkin.

Baked Pumpkin:

Prepare the pumpkin 30 minutes before serving the stew. In a saucepan, melt the butter and add the maple syrup. Bring to a slow boil and add the pumpkin. Remove from heat. Transfer mixture to a buttered, covered casserole and bake in preheated 300° oven for 20 minutes.

To use a pumpkin as serving tureen:

Select a pumpkin that will fit in your oven. Remove the top and set aside. Using a large spoon, scrape out the seeds and stringy residue. Preheat the oven to 250°. Place the pumpkin in a sturdy shallow pan. Ladle the stew into the pumpkin, top off with additional red wine, replace the pumpkin top and bake for 1½ to 2 hours or until the meat and vegetables are tender and pumpkin has changed color. Supporting the bottom, place pumpkin on a serving tray, The pumpkin tureen will retain the heat of the stew for several hours. Best of all, it's disposable!

Serves six to eight generously.

1 pound venison, cut in 1" cubes and dusted with flour (beef, buffalo, moose, elk etc. may be substituted)
1 pound duck thighs, boned, cut in 1" cubes and dusted with flour
½ pound pork loin cut in 1" cubes and dusted with flour
½ pound spicy sausage sliced ¾" thick
¼ pound sweet butter
1 Tablespoon minced garlic
1 large onion, minced
3 stalks celery, chopped
1 cup red wine
1 cup beef or chicken stock
1 cup peeled potato, cut in ¾" cubes
1 cup turnips, cut in ¾" cubes
1 cup rutabaga, cut in ¾" cubes
1 cup baby carrots
1 cup peas
16 ounces stewed tomatoes
2 bay leaves
½ teaspoon basil
¼ teaspoon oregano
2 Tablespoons brown sugar
2 teaspoons salt

Baked Pumpkin:
2 cups raw pumpkin (or squash) cut in 1" cubes
¼ pound butter
¼ cup maple syrup or honey

Pork on the Wild Side

Fresh, fluffy German spaetzle noodles form the wavy base for this unusual combination of textures and symphony of flavors. Taste the spicy wild game sausage mixed with marinated apricots, added for sweetness. Encore! Encore!

Cut a teardrop-shaped pocket in each chop. Place a pork chop on a cutting board with the bone to the left if you are right-handed. Locate the horizontal and vertical center of the chop. Insert the tip of a very sharp boning knife almost to the bone. Cut forward, pulling back on the knife, cutting almost to the outside front edge. Without removing the knife, turn the blade over and repeat this process for the bottom half of the tear-drop pocket. The outside opening should be no larger than 1" in length.

Remove the casing from the sausage. Stuff ¾ of a link in each pocket. Insert a drained apricot and then another ¾ sausage link.

Dust the chops with dry rub mixture and grill or pan sear 2 to 3 minutes on each side. Place chops in a baking dish, add ¼" water and cover with foil. Bake for 20 minutes at 350°.

Serve with a rich brown sauce (see p. 96), spaetzle and fresh vegetables.

Serves four.

*To expand recipe, allow 1 chop and 1½ ounce sausage per serving.

Spaetzle:
In a stainless steel bowl, mix together all ingredients until smooth. Let rest at least one hour. Bring 3 quarts light chicken stock or water to a boil. Force flour mixture through the large holes of a grater or spaetzle maker into the stock. As spaetzle floats, remove to a heated covered dish. Drizzle with melted butter and serve.

4 center-cut pork chops (bone-in), 1¾" thick

6 links (2 ounces) fresh wild game sausage (spicy pheasant, venison, or spicy Italian, etc.)

4 dried apricots marinated in 4 Tablespoons dry sherry

Dry Rub Seasoning:
1 Tablespoon paprika
1 teaspoon granulated garlic
1 teaspoon white pepper
½ teaspoon cayenne pepper
1 Tablespoon salt
1 teaspoon granulated onion

Spaetzle:
2 cups flour
3 eggs
½ cup cream or milk
1½ teaspoon salt
1 teaspoon nutmeg
3 quarts light chicken stock or water

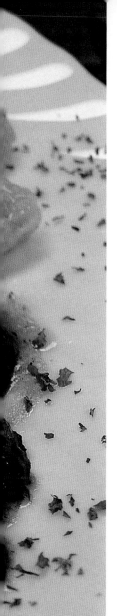

Wild Game Sauerbraten

This is traditional German cooking at its best. A wonderful, substantial meal that is perfect served in Fall or Winter when the cold outdoors calls for something to warm the heart.

Prepare the marinade two to three days ahead, as follows: In a 2-quart saucepan, combine red wine, vinegar, water, onion, peppercorns, juniper berries and bay leaf. Bring to a boil. Cool this mixture to room temperature. Place the meat in a deep crock or stainless steel pan and pour the marinade over it. Marinade should reach halfway up the side of the meat. If not, add red wine. Turn the meat to coat and cover the pan with plastic wrap. Refrigerate for 2 to 3 days, turning the meat 2 to 3 times per day.

Remove the meat from the marinade and pat dry with lint-free towels. Strain marinade into a bowl. Discard onion and spices.

In a heavy 4- to 5-quart flame-proof casserole, sauté the bacon to render the fat. Remove bacon from casserole and reserve for sauce. Add the butter to the casserole. Over high heat, brown the meat on all sides. Remove the meat and sauté onion, carrot and celery, stirring constantly for 3 to 5 minutes. Sprinkle vegetables with flour and cook until flour begins to color. Slowly add strained marinade, stirring constantly, and bring to a boil. Return meat to the casserole. Cover and bake in a 350° preheated oven for 2 hours or until fork tender. Cool to room temperature and refrigerate overnight.

Skim fat from cooking liquid. Remove meat and carve into ¼" to ⅜" slices. Fold the meat slices in half and arrange in overlapping layers in a baking dish. Heat the cooking liquid and add the ginger snap crumbs, beef or vegetable stock and sherry. Stir until slightly thickened. Strain sauce through a fine sieve, pressing as much liquid as possible from the vegetables. Simmer sauce over low heat until thickened and adjust seasoning to taste. Spoon sauce over meat slices and heat in a 300° oven for 15 minutes. Serve with spaetzle (p. 59) and spicy red cabbage (p. 48).

Serves six to eight.

Marinade:
½ **cup dry red wine**
½ **cup red wine vinegar**
2 **cups cold water**
1 **medium onion, peeled and thinly sliced**
8 **peppercorns, crushed**
4 **juniper berries, crushed (optional)**
2 **to 3 bay leaves**

4 **pounds boneless wild game roast (venison, moose, buffalo, etc.), preferably top or bottom round or rump, trimmed of all fat (beef may be substituted)**
4 **ounces sweet butter**
¼ **pound bacon – diced**
½ **cup finely chopped onion**
½ **cup finely chopped carrot**
½ **cup finely chopped celery**
2 **Tablespoons flour**
½ **cup ginger snap crumbs**
1 **cup beef or vegetable stock**
1 **cup cream sherry**

Poached Venison Shank with Dill Cream Sauce

The lean, flavorful meat in this recipe is cooked non-traditionally and complemented with a soothing cream sauce. The dill provides just the right amount of tang, and proves that wild can be elegant.

Place the venison shank in a deep sauté or saucepan large enough to accommodate meat in one layer. Arrange leek, carrot, fennel, dill, onion, peppercorn and bay leaf on top.

In a stainless steel bowl, mix together red wine vinegar, white wine, salt, white pepper and sugar. Pour mixture over venison. Add water to cover meat. Poach over medium heat until meat is fork tender.

In a medium saucepan, prepare a roux by melting 4 Tablespoons butter and then whisking in 2 Tablespoons flour over low heat. Cook until mixture is "blonde" in color.

Carefully remove meat from pan. Cover and keep warm in 150° oven. Strain broth and reserve, discarding the vegetables.

Whisk 4 cups of broth into the roux. Cook over medium heat until sauce is reduced by 10 percent. Whisk in ½ cup heavy cream. Remove from heat and stir in ¾ cup chopped fresh dill. Keep sauce warm over low heat.

Boil potatoes until tender. Add leeks, carrots, fennel and onion. Poach until vegetables are al dente.

Plate 2 shanks per serving. Arrange vegetables on each plate. Ladle sauce over vegetables and meat.

Serves four.

8 pieces venison shank (2 pieces per serving); veal shank may be substituted
four 3" lengths of leek, quartered lengthwise
4 carrots, peeled and cut in quarters
1 fennel bulb, sliced in ⅓" pieces
3-4 sprigs fresh dill
1 large onion, cut in ⅓" slices
24-30 peppercorns
2-3 bay leaves
⅓ cup red wine vinegar
1 cup white wine
1 teaspoon salt
½ teaspoon white pepper
1 Tablespoon sugar
4 Tablespoons butter
2 Tablespoons flour
½ cup heavy cream
¾ cup chopped fresh dill
2 cups julienne leeks
1 cup carrots, peeled and cut in ribbons with a vegetable peeler
12 small ("B" size) red potatoes
1 fennel bulb, cut in ½" slices
1 large onion, cut in ½" slices

Venison Stroganoff

Northwoods' dwellers have long known that venison, like other game meats, is high in protein and virtually free of fat and cholesterol. But for years, they kept the secret of its unique and delicate flavor. Would folks eat it just because it's good for them? Venison's taste and texture is a superb complement to the creamy, barely tangy sauce in this traditional stroganoff.

In a heavy 3-quart covered casserole, brown the venison in ¼ pound butter. Add the onions and remaining butter. Cook 5 minutes.

Mix together stock, tomato purée, salt and pepper. Add to meat mixture along with mushrooms. Simmer 30 to 45 minutes. Stir in the sour cream and adjust seasoning to taste, being careful not to boil. Serve over buttered noodles or steamed rice.

Serves six to eight.

2 pounds venison tenderloin cut in thin ribbons, approximately 1" x 2" x ¼" (beef may be substituted)
½ pound sweet butter
2 cups finely chopped onion
2 cups beef, veal or venison stock
2 cups stewed tomatoes, puréed and strained to remove seeds
½ teaspoon salt
⅛ teaspoon white pepper
1½ pounds button mushrooms, stems removed
2 cups sour cream

Barbecued Goose

Barbecued goose? Henry says, "I know, I know." Just trust him on this. When Henry lived in San Francisco back in 1983, he entered this sauce in The San Francisco Examiner's "Best Barbecue Sauce" contest. He won. The mild, mouth-watering tang makes this sauce a winner. Plus, the mahogany glazed presentation is winning converts across the Northwoods. So, go ahead. Barbecue your goose.

1 pound raw goose per serving

Barbecue Sauce:

In a 2-quart sauté or saucepan, melt the butter over medium heat. Add the onion and garlic and sauté until the onions are translucent. Add the dry spices and continue cooking for 3 minutes, stirring constantly.

Cut the oranges in half and squeeze the juice into the pan. Reserve the orange rinds. Simmer 2 minutes. Add the catsup, molasses and vinegar and mix thoroughly. Bring mixture to a boil. Reduce heat to low and add the orange rinds. Cover and simmer one hour. Remove the orange rinds and reserve for stuffing the goose.

Goose:

Preheat oven to 450°. Remove excess fat from body cavity. Season cavity with salt and pepper and stuff with orange rinds from barbecue sauce.

Season outside of goose with Dry Rub Seasoning.

Place goose in roasting pan, breast side down on a rack. Reduce oven heat to 350°. Cook, uncovered, 20 minutes per pound. Halfway through the cooking time, turn the goose breast side up. Baste with barbecue sauce during the last 30 minutes of cooking time.

Barbecue Sauce:
¼ pound butter
1 large onion, diced
4 cloves garlic, finely minced
¼ teaspoon oregano
¼ teaspoon cumin
¼ teaspoon crushed rosemary
¼ teaspoon salt
⅛ teaspoon pepper
⅛ teaspoon ginger
5-6 Tablespoons chili powder
4 cups catsup
6 oranges
½ cup dark molasses
⅛ cup vinegar

Dry Rub Seasoning—combine:
2 Tablespoons salt
¼ cup dried onion
1 Tablespoon cayenne pepper
1 Tablespoon white pepper
2 Tablespoons paprika
2 Tablespoons dried basil
1 Tablespoon dry mustard
1 teaspoon ground cumin
1 Tablespoon granulated garlic

Lake Trout en Croute

Too fancy? Too difficult? Nonsense! This dish is surprisingly simple to produce. Let the artist in you create and delight your guests with your handiwork as they savor the steamy, licorice flavor of this dish.

Sauté bacon, onion and garlic in 1 Tablespoon butter until bacon is slightly rendered and onion is translucent. Remove pan from heat and stir in the cheese, spinach and Pernod. Season to taste with salt and pepper. Chill mixture at least one hour before proceeding.

Place trout filets, skin side down, on work surface. Place ¼ cup spinach mixture on each filet and roll into a cylinder. Chill at least one hour before proceeding.

Roll out one piece puff pastry large enough to cover a trout roll overlapping by 1½" on all sides. Roll another piece of puff pastry for the base, extending 1½" on each side. Place trout on base pastry and brush edges of pastry with beaten egg. Drape the top piece of pastry over the trout. Trim edges to uniform shape and seal by roll folding the edges.

Cut decorative shapes from the remaining pastry piece. Brush top of pastry with beaten egg and place cut out on top of each trout packet.

Bake in a preheated 400° oven for 20 minutes or until golden brown. Serve with hollandaise sauce.

Serves four.

4 6-ounce pieces center cut lake trout filet, trimmed of all fat (salmon may be substituted)
3 slices bacon, cut in ¼" dice
1 Tablespoon sweet butter
3 Tablespoons diced onion
1 clove garlic, minced
2 Tablespoons shredded asiago cheese
2 cups steamed spinach, all water removed
1 ounce Pernod or Pastisse (or licorice flavored cordial)
9 puff pastry pieces, 5" x 5"

Mussels, Chicken and Crayfish

(Shown at left with shrimp substituted for crayfish)

Salty, robust fishermen scour the ocean off the coast of Maine for plump mussels which form the heart of this tasty dish. Serving suggestion from New England's Northwoods: a crackling fireplace, a crusty loaf of bread, sweet butter and a flagon of rich, red wine.

In a large pot, steam the mussels in white wine with 1 Tablespoon garlic. The mussels are cooked when their shells open. Strain and reserve the cooking broth. Remove mussels from shells. Save the shells for garnish.

In a 4-quart pot, sauté the bacon over medium heat until opaque. Reduce heat to low and add the onion and green pepper. Sauté until onions are translucent. Add the chicken, potatoes, 1 Tablespoon garlic and Italian seasoning and sauté 5 minutes. Mix together the veloute sauce, clam juice and reserved mussel broth and add to the chicken vegetable mixture. Add crayfish meat and mussels and simmer over low heat 20 to 30 minutes. Adjust seasoning with salt and pepper. Finish the sauce by stirring in pieces of sweet butter.

Serve over steamed rice or pasta. Garnish with tomato and mussel shells.

Serves six to eight.

- 2 pounds black mussels, rinsed and de-bearded
- 1 pound chicken breast, skinned and de-boned, cut into ¾" dice (chopped clams may be substituted)
- ½ pound cooked crayfish meat (shrimp may be substituted)
- 1 cup white wine
- 2 Tablespoons minced garlic
- 4 pieces thick-sliced bacon
- 1 cup green pepper cut in medium dice
- 1 large onion cut in medium dice
- 2 large potatoes, peeled and diced
- 1 teaspoon Italian seasoning
- 1 quart veloute sauce (see page 75 and double the recipe)
- 2 cups clam juice
- ½ pound sweet butter
- 1 cup roma tomatoes, seeded and diced

Oven Poached Lake Perch

A classic technique — poaching — lends an elegant twist to the usually pan-fried perch. The result: a moister-than-most fish presented as an attractive entrée.

Butter a large oven-proof dish. Mix together carrot, celery, onion and sun-dried tomato and distribute evenly in the bottom of the baking dish. Sprinkle with basil. Fold perch filets in half, skin side in, and place in the dish, overlapping slightly. Add clam juice and cover the fish with buttered parchment paper.

Bake in a preheated 350° oven for 15 to 20 minutes. Strain cooking liquid into a saucepan and return fish to oven to keep warm. Over medium heat, reduce liquid by one-half. Add cream and gradually whisk in butter. Adjust seasoning with salt and pepper. Just before serving, sauce the fish.

Serves six.

2 pounds fresh or frozen lake perch (any white fish, such as sole, may be substituted)
1 cup julienne-cut carrot
1 cup julienne-cut celery
1 cup thinly sliced sweet onion
¼ cup thinly sliced sun-dried tomato
1 teaspoon fresh basil
2 cups clam juice
1 cup heavy cream
¼ pound sweet butter

Shore Lunch

Imagine arriving at the lake at dawn, fishing until noon and then dining on this wonderful repast from the fruits of the morning's labor! The Shore Lunch combines the best of all worlds — the great outdoors, the challenge of landing that trophy fish, and the unbelievable gourmet experience of freshly caught fish, prepared and cooked on the spot. This is what "fresh fish" is all about.

Typically, a Northwoods' Shore Lunch consists of fried potatoes, baked beans, a salad and the often illusive fresh fish (fried). The following is our version of an upscale Shore Lunch.

Prepare the fire. When coals are gray, level the coals and place the grate over the fire.

Boil water for coffee.

In one frying pay, mix together the canned beans and marinated dry fruit. Place on grate over the coolest part of the fire. Heat through, stirring occasionally. When hot, cover with foil and remove from the fire.

Heat approximately ¼" butter or olive oil in a frying pan. Add sliced potatoes and brown, seasoning to taste with salt and pepper. Add the sausage, sliced. Heat through until potatoes are tender. Cover with foil and move to a cooler part of the fire.

Pour evaporated milk in a plastic bag (reserving some for your coffee). Place breading mix in another plastic bag. Coat fish filets with evaporated milk, then breading mix.

Place filets in a hot frying pan with ¼" butter or olive oil. Fry until golden brown, turning once.

Serve the mussel salad as a first course followed by plates of fish, potatoes and sausage, and beans. Serve 1-2 filets per person.

The success of any Shore Lunch is based upon careful preparation and provisioning. The night before your trip, pack the following items in waterproof containers:

charcoal, charcoal lighter and matches
3 large cast iron frying pans
1 roll heavy duty aluminum foil
1 wire grate
1 long blade spatula
2 long handled serving spoons
heavy paper plates, disposable utensils, paper napkins, coffee cups
1 gallon water and dish soap
salt and pepper
pot holders
coffee pot, instant coffee, sugar, lemon
large plastic bags

1-2 large fish filet per person
1 large baked potato per person, sliced
1 can unsweetened evaporated milk
prepared breading mix of your choice
½ Tablespoon dried apricots or apples (marinated in 1 Tablespoon sherry) per person
marinated mussel salad (see page 37)
baked beans (canned)
pre-cooked bratwurst or Italian sausage (just in case the fish are not home)
cranberry tartar sauce (see page 94)
butter and olive oil

Smoked Salmon & Chives in Cream Sauce

Start with the pinkest of salmon, preferably Pacific Ocean fresh. This simple delight is guaranteed to please.

Veloute White Sauce:

In a stainless steel saucepan, melt butter over low heat. Whisk in flour and slowly add stock and cream until well blended. Stirring constantly, heat sauce until thickened. Add a pinch of nutmeg and season to taste with salt and pepper. Makes 1 cup.

Julienne slice salmon across the grain. Add the salmon and chives to the heated white sauce and simmer ten minutes. Serve over fresh pasta or steamed rice. Garnish with diced tomato.

For each serving:

6 ounces sliced lox salmon
1 Tablespoon fresh minced chives
½ cup seeded roma tomatoes, diced
1 cup veloute white sauce

Veloute white sauce:

1 Tablespoons sweet butter
1 Tablespoons flour
½ cup chicken, veal or fish stock
½ cup heavy cream
nutmeg
salt and pepper

Salmon Roulade

A magnificent presentation with incredible flavors, this recipe showcases salmon. The salmon's incredible natural flavor may be enhanced by serving it with steamed rice, fresh vegetables, or Stewed Pumpkin and Apples (see page 31).

Carefully remove skin and bones from the salmon steaks. Trim fat from the belly flaps. Chill at least one hour.

Mix together spinach, mushrooms and Pernod. Season to taste with salt and pepper and refrigerate at least one hour.

Mix together the marinade ingredients.

Place a salmon steak on a square of plastic wrap. Place approximately 2 Tablespoons of chilled spinach/mushroom mixture on the center cavity of the salmon steak. Wrap the steak around the mixture pinwheel fashion. Flatten slightly and sprinkle with 1 Tablespoon of the marinade. Wrap in plastic wrap and refrigerate at least 2 hours. Remove the plastic wrap and place the roulade in a buttered pan. Bake in a preheated 400° oven for 10 to 15 minutes.

Serves four.

4 salmon steaks, approximately 1" thick
½ cup steamed spinach (moisture removed)
¼ cup blanched mushrooms (cut ¼" x 1")
1 Tablespoon Pernod

Marinade:
½ cup Chardonnay or other dry white wine
2 Tablespoons lemon juice
1 Tablespoon dill weed (preferably fresh)

Desserts

Fresh Berry Napoleons

Berry pickers flock to the Northwoods each summer, sharing the territory with fruit-loving bears. Layer fresh berries into the rich ingredients of this recipe for a lyrical fruit sensation that will amaze your guests.

Place the puff pastry rounds on a baking sheet. Prick each with a fork. Moisten with a pastry brush dipped in cold water and sprinkle with sugar. Bake in a preheated 400° oven for 10-15 minutes or until brown and crispy. Remove to a rack and cool completely.

Toss together blueberries, strawberries and blackberries. Add the Triple Sec. Refrigerate at least one hour.

In a stainless steel bowl, using an electric mixer, blend together the cheese, sugar, rum and raspberry liqueur. Slowly add the cream until you achieve the consistency of butter cream frosting. Transfer the mixture to a pastry bag fitted with a #22 open star tip.

To assemble, pipe a dot of cheese mixture in the center of each dessert plate. Gently press a puff pastry round on the cheese to secure the base. Pipe a band of cheese mixture on the edge of the puff pastry round. Fill the center with fruit mixture. Repeat this process with two more layers. Garnish the plate with fresh raspberries.

Serves six.

1 pint blueberries
1 pint strawberries, sliced
1 pint blackberries
1 pint raspberries
2 Tablespoons Triple Sec
11" x 15" commercially prepared puff pastry sheets cut into 3" rounds; 1 sheet yields 18 rounds
1 pound marscapone cheese, softened (domestic cream cheese may be substituted)
2 Tablespoons rum
1 Tablespoon raspberry liqueur
1½ cups heavy cream
¼ cup granulated sugar

Raspberry Crème Brûlée

There's a simple surprise in this version of the classic dessert — the berries inside!

Custard:

In a stainless steel bowl, using an electric mixer, beat the egg yolks and vanilla sugar until the mixture falls from the beater in a ribbon. With the beater running, add the scalded cream in a slow steady stream. Place the bowl over a pot of boiling water, reduce heat to medium and cook the mixture, stirring constantly until it coats the back of the spoon. Do not boil! Remove pan from heat. Stir in the lemon zest and raspberry liqueur with softened gelatin.

Set out eight 4-ounce ramekins. Divide 1 pint raspberries among the ramekins, fill with custard to ¼" from the top. Chill at least 3 hours or until set.

One hour before serving, sprinkle the top of each custard evenly with 1 Tablespoon sugar. Using a torch, caramelize the sugar — begin at the center and move to the outer edge in concentric circles. Return ramekins to the refrigerator.

Garnish the serving plates with fresh raspberries and ginger snap cookies.

Serves eight.

Vanilla Sugar:

Place one piece vanilla bean in the bottom of a 2-quart jar. Cover with 1 cup sugar. Repeat this process using remaining vanilla bean pieces and sugar. Cover. Let sit for 1 week, shaking jar occasionally.

8 egg yolks
¼ cup vanilla sugar (see below)
2¾ cups heavy cream, scalded
3 Tablespoons raspberry liqueur
2 teaspoons lemon zest, finely minced
8 Tablespoons sugar
2½ pints fresh raspberries
1 Tablespoon gelatin softened in the raspberry liqueur

Vanilla Sugar:
4 cups granulated sugar
2 vanilla beans, split lengthwise

Wild Rice Cake

This delectable cake blends a utilitarian Northwoods staple, wild rice, with sweet, melt-in-your-mouth ingredients reminiscent of traditional plum pudding. The combination of soft and crunchy textures and sweet and nutty flavors makes this a smash.

Combine flour with salt and baking powder.

Combine cooked wild rice with walnut pieces (for a smoother textured cake, process rice and walnuts one or two pulse cycles in food processor with steel blade).

Cream butter until softened. Add brown sugar. Beat in eggs, one at a time. Add buttermilk, maple favoring and nutmeg. Beat until light and fluffy. Stir in flour mixture until thoroughly mixed. Fold in rice and walnut mixture.

Pour batter into an 8" tube or bundt pan. Bake in 350° oven for about 1 hour. Yields one 8" tube cake. Works well topped with a bourbon custard sauce.

Serves six to eight.

Bourbon Custard Sauce:

Beat 2 egg yolks and the sugar with a wire whisk until the mixture is a pale yellow. Slowly add the bourbon and mix well. Whip the cream until stiff. Fold in vanilla and then the egg mixture into the whipped cream. Makes about 2 cups. Keep refrigerated.

2 cups sifted flour
¼ teaspoon salt
½ teaspoon baking powder
2 cups cooked wild rice (cooked until bloomed) – ½ cup uncooked*
1 cup walnut pieces
½ cup sweet butter
1 cup dark brown sugar
4 eggs
¾ cup buttermilk
1 teaspoon maple flavoring
½ teaspoon nutmeg

Bourbon Custard Sauce:

2 egg yolks
1 cup confectioners' sugar
8 Tablespoons bourbon
1 cup whipping cream
1 teaspoon vanilla

* See page 21 for directions on cooking wild rice.

Pumpkin Cheese Tart with Cranberry Apple Glaze

This inventive dessert first visits the pumpkin patch, stops by the cranberry bog, and raids a few apple trees before becoming a tantalizing tart. Definitely NOT like mother used to make.

In a food processor bowl fitted with a metal blade, cut the butter into the flour by pulsing the blade. Turn the machine on constant power and slowly add the ice water in a steady stream. In less than 30 seconds, a ball will form. Stop the machine. Wrap the dough in plastic wrap and refrigerate at least one hour.

Roll pastry dough into approximately a 13" diameter circle. Line an 11" quiche or tart pan (with removable bottom) with the pastry dough. Gently press the pastry into the fluted rim. Trim excess from top. Line the pastry with wax paper and weight down with dry beans or uncooked rice. Bake in a preheated 350° oven for 15-20 minutes. Remove from oven. Remove waxed paper and beans/rice. Cool.

In a food processor fitted with a steel blade, blend together the pumpkin pie mix, cheese, sugar, eggs, orange peel and juice until smooth and silky. Pour mixture into pie shell. Bake at 350° for 30-40 minutes or until a toothpick inserted in the center comes out clean. Cool on a rack and glaze.

In a 2-quart saucepan, heat the juice, rum and teriyaki sauce to boiling. Reduce by half. Add cornstarch/water mixture. Reduce heat and stir until thickened. Cool before glazing tart.

Serves eight.

Pastry Dough:
1 ⅓ cups flour
¼ pound cold sweet butter, cut into small pieces
¼ cup ice water

Filling:
1 16-ounce can pumpkin pie mix
8 ounces mascarpone or cream cheese
1 cup sugar
2 large eggs
1 Tablespoon grated orange peel
½ Tablespoon lemon juice

Cranberry Apple Glaze:
4 cups cranapple juice
1 Tablespoon dark rum
12 Tablespoon teriyaki sauce
1 Tablespoon cornstarch mixed with 3 Tablespoons water

Wild Rice Pudding with Raspberry Sauce

Wild rice, sturdier than "regular" rice, provides the crunch and the nutty flavor to the otherwise silken texture of this delicious confection.

In a 2-quart saucepan, dissolve gelatin in water. Add sugar and salt. Cook over medium heat until sugar is dissolved, stirring constantly. Do not boil. Stir in 2 cups cream, rice, vanilla, cinnamon and nutmeg. Cool mixture in an ice bath, stirring occasionally, until mixture begins to set (about 15 minutes).

Fold whipped cream into rice mixture. Pour into ungreased 1½-quart mold. Cover and refrigerate until firm, 4 to 6 hours. Unmold and serve with Raspberry Sauce.

In a 2-quart saucepan, mix together jam, liqueur, sugar, water and salt. Bring slowly to a boil, stirring constantly. Remove from heat and strain to remove seeds. Return sauce to pan and bring to a boil. Mix cornstarch with 1 cup cold water. Stir into boiling sauce until thickened. Cool and refrigerate until service.

Serves six to eight.

4 cups cooked wild rice*
¾ cup sugar
¾ cup water
¼ teaspoon salt
2 cups heavy cream
2 envelopes unflavored gelatin
2 teaspoons vanilla
¼ teaspoon cinnamon
¼ teaspoon nutmeg
1 cup heavy cream whipped to stiff peaks

Raspberry Sauce:
16-ounce jar raspberry jam
4 ounces raspberry liqueur
2 cups water
2 cups sugar
1 teaspoon salt
⅓ cup cornstarch
1 cup cold water

* See page 21 for directions on cooking wild rice.

Applesauce Carrot Cake

The combined vegetable and fruit flavors team-up in this rich and moist cake. The best comfort food treat west of The Pemigewasset Wilderness.

Beat together eggs, brown sugar, butter and vanilla. Sift together flour, baking soda, salt and cinnamon. Add to egg mixture. Fold in applesauce, walnuts and carrots. Pour into ungreased bundt pan. Bake at 350° for 60 minutes or until a toothpick inserted in the center comes out clean.

Combine the ingredients for the frosting. Add heavy cream as needed to bring to the consistency of a glaze.

Serves eight.

1 cup butter
3 eggs
2 cups light brown sugar
1½ teaspoons vanilla
2 cups flour
2 teaspoons baking soda
½ teaspoon salt
2 teaspoons cinnamon
1 cup applesauce
1 cup chopped walnuts
2 cups shredded carrots (½ pound)

Frosting:
3 ounces softened cream cheese
¼ cup softened butter
 dash of salt
½ pound confectioners' sugar
1½ teaspoons vanilla

Sauces

Cranberry Mustard

Something a little different. Sweet, spicy and pungent. A wonderful gift for a special friend.

2 cups cooked cranberries (about 1
    pound uncooked)
⅓ cup whole mustard seed
⅓ cup boiling water
⅓ cup dry mustard
⅓ cup boiling water
1 cup cider vinegar
⅓ cup dark brown sugar
1½ teaspoon salt
1 teaspoon onion powder
½ teaspoon garlic powder
¼ teaspoon cinnamon
¼ teaspoon allspice
½ teaspoon ground cloves
3 Tablespoons light corn syrup

In two separate glass or ceramic bowls, combine mustard seed with ⅓ cup boiling water in one and the dry mustard with ⅓ cup boiling water in the other. Let stand for 10 minutes.

Combine remainder of ingredients in a 2-quart stainless steel saucepan. Heat over medium heat to boiling. Add mustard mixtures and simmer, covered, for 5 minutes.

Process the mixture in a food processor or blender until the mustard seeds are crushed. Pour into glass or ceramic containers with tight-fitting lids and refrigerate. Yields 3 to 4 cups.

Cranberry Mustard Vinaigrette

Fresh and pungent, this dressing is an excellent choice for mixed field greens or spinach salad.

⅓ cup cranberry mustard
¾ cup red wine vinegar
2 teaspoons salt
½ teaspoon white pepper
⅓ cup olive oil

In a ceramic or glass bowl, blender or food processor, combine mustard, vinegar, salt and pepper. Slowly add olive oil, while processing/blending, until emulsified. Pour into glass or ceramic container with tight-fitting lid and refrigerate.

Cranberry Tarter Sauce

Cranberries — not just for Thanksgiving anymore. This sauce is wonderful with fish or deep-fried oysters or as a sandwich condiment.

½ cup cranberry mustard
1 cup mayonnaise
2 Tablespoons sweet pickle relish
2 Tablespoons finely chopped ripe
    olives
2 Tablespoons finely chopped green
    olives
2 Tablespoons finely chopped capers
2 Tablespoons finely chopped fresh
    parsley
1 Tablespoon fresh lemon juice
Optional:
2 finely chopped hard-boiled eggs

Combine all ingredients – mix well. Refrigerate at least one hour before serving.

Enriched Sauce Veloute

A classic white sauce made from a roux in which a light stock usually takes the place of milk or cream. This sauce is an excellent base for many robust Northwoods' soups and sauces.

2 Tablespoons sweet butter
2 Tablespoons flour
1 cup chicken, veal or fish stock
1 cup heavy cream
nutmeg

In a stainless steel saucepan, melt butter over low heat. Whisk in flour and slowly add stock and cream until well blended. Stirring constantly, heat sauce until thickened. Add a pinch of nutmeg and season to taste with salt and pepper. Yields about 2 cups.

Rich Brown Sauce

1 clove garlic, minced
2 Tablespoons minced onion
3 Tablespoons butter
3 Tablespoons flour
1 cup beef stock
1 cup chicken stock
1 Tablespoon sherry or Madeira wine
1 ounce butter

Sauté garlic and onion in butter until golden. Over low heat, stir in the flour until well blended. Cook the mixture 1 to 2 minutes until slightly brown. Slowly blend in the beef and chicken stock, and bring to a slow boil stirring constantly. Add the wine and season to taste with salt and pepper. Finish the sauce by whisking in 1 ounce butter. Makes about 2 cups.

*Note: If sauce is lumpy or onion and garlic pieces are too large, strain the sauce before serving.

Blackberry and Port Wine Sauce

1 4-ounce jar blackberry jam
4 ounces sugar
4 ounces port wine
2 ounces blackberry brandy
½ cup teriyaki sauce
1 Tablespoons cornstarch

Prepare sauce by mixing the blackberry jam, sugar, port wine and brandy in a 2-quart saucepan. Stirring constantly, bring the mixture to a boil. Reduce heat and simmer for 10 to 15 minutes, stirring occasionally. Strain the mixture into a clean 2-quart saucepan and return to low heat. Mix together cornstarch and teriyaki sauce. Add to blackberry jam mixture and heat until slightly thickened. Yields 1½ pints of sauce.

Suppliers

Earthy Delights
1161 E. Clark Road, Ste. 260
DeWitt, MI 48820
800-367-4709
www.earthy.com
(for wild mushrooms, truffles, wild rice, fruit sauces, edible flowers, nuts & seeds, beans & lentils, fiddlehead fern, spices & fresh herbs)

Uncle Tom's Farm
P.O. Box 42
Gardiner, OR
541-271-5401
email: uncletom@harborside.com
www.uncle-toms-farm.com
(for pheasant, quail, turkey, ducks & geese)

Gourmet Smoked Products
P.O. Box 2667
Lilburn, GA 30048
770-923-8111
www.gourmetsmokedproducts.com
(for wild game, waterfowl, cheese)

Broken Arrow Ranch
800-962-4263
(for venison and other wild game)

Seattle's Finest Exotic Meats
17532 Aurora Ave. N.
Seattle, WA 98133
www.exoticmeats.com
(for exotic meats)